EUREKA!
THE **BIOGRAPHY** OF AN **IDEA**

FIREWORKS

BY LORI HASKINS HOURAN • ILLUSTRATED BY CORINNE CARO

KANEPRESS

AN IMPRINT OF ASTRA BOOKS FOR YOUNG READERS
New York

For fireworks fans everywhere!—LHH

For my wonderful family—CC

Special thanks to Monica Smith, Associate Director,
the Smithsonian's Lemelson Center for the Study
of Invention and Innovation

Library of Congress Cataloging-in-Publication Data

Names: Houran, Lori Haskins, author. | Caro, Corinne, illustrator.
Title: Fireworks : eureka! the biography of an idea / Lori Haskins Houran ;
    illustrated by Corinne Caro.
Description: First edition. | New York : Kane Press, 2024. | Series:
    Eureka! the biography of an idea | Audience: Ages 4-8 | Audience: Grades
    K-1 | Summary: "From the first gunpowder-filled bamboo stalk thrown on
    a bonfire to dazzling overhead multicolor displays of today, Fireworks is
    a fun and informative look at the development of an invention that
    sparks joy"—Provided by publisher.
Identifiers: LCCN 2023026901 (print) | LCCN 2023026902 (ebook) |
    ISBN 9781662670541 (hardcover) | ISBN 9781662651397 (trade paperback) |
    ISBN 9781662651403 (ebk)
Subjects: LCSH: Fireworks—History—Juvenile literature.
Classification: LCC TP300 .H68 2024 (print) | LCC TP300 (ebook) | DDC
    662/.109—dc23/eng/20231002
LC record available at https://lccn.loc.gov/2023026901
LC ebook record available at https://lccn.loc.gov/2023026902

Kane Press
An imprint of Astra Books for Young Readers,
a division of Astra Publishing House
kanepress.com
Printed in Malaysia

10 9 8 7 6 5 4 3 2 1

IT'S JULY 4TH.

Across America, the parades are done. The picnics are packed up. But the party is not over! Crowds of people stare up in the dark, waiting.

Suddenly, the sky erupts with color and noise! A swirl of red. *POP!* A shower of white. *CRACK!* A burst of blue. *BOOM!*

"Ooooh!" the crowd gasps. "Ahhhh!"

CHINA, AROUND 200 CE

Fireworks have been around for over a thousand years.

In ancient China, villagers tossed bamboo stalks into bonfires. The heat made air pockets inside the bamboo pop. *Bang!*

Then Chinese people invented **gunpowder**—a mix of saltpeter, sulfur, and charcoal that explodes when it catches fire.

Someone stuffed gunpowder into the bamboo. Now when the stalks popped, they flashed bright orange sparks, too!

Just like that, fireworks were born.

CHINA, 1200s

Over time, paper tubes replaced the bamboo stalks. People also added paper **fuses**, little tails that dangled from the fireworks. The end of the fuse was set on fire, and the flame traveled along the fuse until it lit the firework.

Thanks to fuses, fireworks didn't have to be thrown into bonfires anymore. Some people strung them on poles to make sparkly displays. Others aimed them at the sky!

Fireworks became part of important celebrations in China, like Lunar New Year. Their big booms and bright flashes were said to scare away evil spirits.

ITALY, 1200s

Marco Polo, an Italian explorer, saw fireworks
in China. He had a feeling people in Italy would
love them, so he took some home.

Marco Polo was right! The biggest firework fans? Royal
families. Kings and queens across Europe started setting off
fireworks to celebrate everything from birthdays to battles.

GERMANY, 1500s

The shows got even better when inventor Johann Schmidlap came along. He created the "step rocket" to shoot fireworks higher.

First a large rocket took off, carrying a small rocket. The small rocket held fireworks inside. When the big rocket burned out, the small one.

e small rocket kept going— p, up, up.

The fireworks

finally erupted,

showering the sky!

9

ENGLAND, 1575

Nobody adored fireworks more than Queen Elizabeth I of England. An earl named Robert Dudley wanted to marry Elizabeth. He ordered a grand fireworks show to impress her.

The show had it all. Blazing rockets. A giant wheel of sparks. Even a fire-breathing dragon! The dragon, made of wood and paper, was stuffed with fireworks that burst from its mouth.

Wow!

But things did not go to plan. The rockets landed
on nearby houses . . . and burned them down.
Elizabeth had to pay for the damage.
  She did not marry Robert.

ENGLAND AND RUSSIA, 1600s

As Robert Dudley found out, putting on a fireworks show was difficult and dangerous.

In England, workers covered themselves with fresh leaves to protect themselves from falling sparks. They got the nickname "green men."

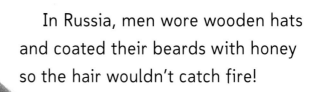

In Russia, men wore wooden hats and coated their beards with honey so the hair wouldn't catch fire!

AMERICA, 1777

Fireworks crossed the sea to America. On July 4, 1777—a year after the Declaration of Independence was signed—Americans enjoyed a splendid display in Philadelphia, Pennsylvania.

It was the first July 4th celebration!

The fireworks weren't red, white, and blue. They were orange.
Up to then, *all* fireworks were orange—the color of fire.
That was about to change.

ITALY, 1830s

In the 1800s, many skilled firework-makers lived in Italy. Around 1830, the Italians made an incredible discovery.

By adding minerals to gunpowder, they could create fireworks in a rainbow of shades. Sodium made yellow. Barium made green. Strontium made red.

These colorful new fireworks took off all over the world!

15

••• KA-BOOM! •••
HOW DO FIREWORKS WORK?

1. First, the **main fuse** is lit. Experts use a computer to send an electric signal that lights the fuse.

main fuse

second fuse

4. The explosion lights a **second fuse**, inside the firework's **shell**. This fuse burns slowly, to give the firework time to reach the sky.

shell

2. The flame travels along the fuse to the **lift charge**—a packet of gunpowder at the base of the firework.

5. The shell holds **stars**, small pellets of chemicals and minerals that give fireworks their color. When the second fuse finishes burning . . .

lift charge

stars

3. The lift charge explodes, pushing the firework into the sky.

Ka-BOOM! The shell breaks. The stars fly out
and burst, lighting up the sky!

AUSTRALIA, 1995

Over the next 150 years, fireworks got fancier. Countries put on bigger and bigger events, especially for New Year's Eve.

On December 31, 1995, Australia showed its fireworks on TV. Viewers around the world admired the glittery display over Sydney Harbour Bridge.

UNITED ARAB EMIRATES, 2010

Not to be outdone, the United Arab Emirates started its own show in 2010. Every year since then, a flurry of fireworks has burst from the Burj Khalifa—the tallest building on Earth!

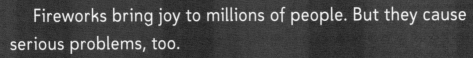

Fireworks bring joy to millions of people. But they cause serious problems, too.

First off, fireworks are dangerous.

Since the 1980s, experts have used computers to set off firework shows from a safe distance. But accidents still happen—often to folks lighting fireworks at home. Each year, thousands of people go to the hospital with firework injuries.

KIDS SHOULD NEVER TOUCH FIREWORKS OF ANY KIND.

Fireworks cause pollution, too. The gunpowder inside creates smoke and ash.

The Walt Disney company found a clever way to cut back on pollution. In 2004, the company started launching fireworks with air instead of gunpowder!

The air is **compressed**, or forced into a tight space. Then the firework is added on top. When the air is released, it thrusts the firework into the sky.

23

Another problem? Fireworks are noisy. Many people and animals don't like the loud cracks and bangs.

Companies have started offering "silent fireworks." They aren't really silent—they still make *some* noise—but they're much quieter than regular fireworks.

The town of Collechio, Italy passed a law in 2015 that only silent fireworks can be set off there. Towns in other countries are following their lead.

Cleaner, quieter fireworks just might be the way of the future. There's another option. Drones could become the new fireworks! At the Tokyo Olympics in 2021, hundreds of tiny, bright drones whizzed through the air. They drew dazzling designs over the city.

For centuries, people have lit up the sky to celebrate
festivals,
ball games,
and holidays.
Chances are, we'll do it for centuries more!

29

FIREWORK FACTS

• Chinese monks may have invented gunpowder by accident while they were trying to make medicine.

• Warriors in ancient China used fireworks as weapons. They aimed bamboo "fire arrows" at their enemies.

• The Nestlé company made a chocolate firework in 2002! When it exploded, it released 132 pounds of candies.

• The hardest color to make with fireworks? Bright blue. That's because copper—the mineral used in blue fireworks—doesn't last long in high heat.

• Firework makers have to wear cotton clothes—right down to their undies! Other fabrics cause static electricity that can set off fireworks.

STATIC-FREE ZONE